17 Love Poems
with No Despair

Also by BJ Ward

Landing in New Jersey with Soft Hands

17 Love Poems with No Despair

BJ Ward

North Atlantic Books
Berkeley, California

17 Love Poems with No Despair

Published by
North Atlantic Books
P.O. Box 12327
Berkeley, California 94712

Front and back cover photographs by Miss Heather Lea Poole
Cover and book design by Catherine Campaigne
Printed in the United States of America

17 Love Poems with No Despair is sponsored by the Society for the Study of Native Arts and Sciences, a nonprofit educational corporation whose goals are to develop an educational and crosscultural perspective linking various scientific, social, and artistic fields; to nurture a holistic view of arts, sciences, humanities, and healing; and to publish and distribute literature on the relationship of mind, body, and nature.

Library of Congress Cataloging-in-Publication Data
Ward, BJ
    17 love poems with no despair / BJ Ward.
      p. cm.
    ISBN 1-55643-243-7
    1. Love poetry, American.   I. Title.
    PS3573.A693A13   1997
    811'.54—dc21   96-39838
                                  CIP

3 4 5 6 7 8 9 / 07 06 05 04 03 02

Gratitudes

Continued gratitude to all my teachers, great and small.

Much thanks to the New Jersey State Council on the Arts/Department of State for a Distinguished Artist Fellowship that helped in the composition of many of these poems. Thanks also to the English Department at Syracuse University for the fellowships and scholarship that enabled me to study at the Creative Writing Program there.

My thanks to Edwin Romond, Charles Rafferty, and Nickole Ingram for their close attention to many of these poems.

Thanks to the editorial staff at *Exit 13* where "The Apple Orchard in October" originally appeared in an earlier form.

A tip of the hat to the Carroll family for their assistance in creating the covers of this book and *Landing in New Jersey with Soft Hands*. Thanks also to Ben Lapinski and all the brothers and sisters at the IKA for their unfailing support and assistance.

Deep gratitude, of course, to Pablo—Neftalí Ricardo Reyes Basoalto—whose writing at the beginning of this century has made room for these—and many other—love poems at the end. I write in ravishing shadows.

Thanks Heath.

Contents

Not Rose Petals

Our love is not rose petals
or Valentine candy—
it is dirt and sand
    and the coarse pebbles in a shallow brook.

It is on our clothes, in our hair—
it is the foundation we walk on
and the soil we roll in
    all night long
    when we're away from each other.

It is not rinsed out by any rain
    or shower—
        we are so filthy with our love
that water will only run over it,
    not run it out.

Our love is dirt and sand
    and coarse pebbles in a shallow brook.

Whatever water hits us,
    our love makes it sing
        in its running.

Its song is the sound of this book.

This Is Right In Front of You

You better ignore this.
You better staple your eyes shut
and put pot-lids over your ears
and pinch your nose with vice grips
and cement your mouth shut
with real cement and while
you're at it or in it or whatever
cut off your hands for good measure

and when you are alone in your head
and the outside world is just a remote country
across a dark sea and your thoughts
line up in front of you, colorful rowboats
on the unsettled water, and when you see
the gigantic word they spell
is the same word you could never say
for fear its echoes would haunt you
out of your comfortable but shaky house—

when you see that you are in love
will you call my name then?

Yes, you better ignore this
or your life will collapse from beneath
you and you and your glass of iced tea
will have no map to direct you
to safety.
                    But if you don't ignore this
and are floating in the space between us
look at the stars overhead. Find the brightest

and pin any hope you have onto it.
Let your hope dribble in one long stream
back to the mountains of the earth.
And when the moon swings through this line,
lean towards that point. Form a long shadow
across our space and I will walk on it
as I always have—walking on your darkness
toward your still red lips where I will break
the cement, free the tools that have maintained
your careful face, expose your ears to the slight music
of the stars burning around us, open your eyes and,
yes, I will lift up your hands
                              and give them back to you.

Together we can become a library
of illegible knowledge, read the ancient scriptures
inscribed around the skin cells of our bellies,
the old writings that were born into our irises
which are as round as planets not yet walked on.
We can wall ourselves into our own dumb love
and together we will ignore everything. Everything.
No research will be done, just a deep reading,
unearthing a history that is happening now.

Her Hands Have Turned Into Fists

What force they contain!
I try to open them
and find they resist
quite beautifully—
they've closed on the lines
gypsies have marked
her life with—
closed on the layer
of skin that grew yes-
terday, closed
closed on the echoes
they'd contain if I
whispered my loves
into her palms.
Those echoes would resound
quite beautifully into
the ears of the small
animals her bones have turned
into—large eyes and tiny
teeth, sharp enough
to see and chew what
almost isn't there.
Yes, I would like to
unclose them but she
just squeezes tighter,
the fingers whitening,
her skin receding,

the whole of her hands
becoming a ghost
around what she is
not holding.

Losing Myself

I've tried diners and train stations.
　　I've tried secluded mountains
and the bottoms of coffee mugs,

but nothing has matched the compacted loneliness
　　inside me like the density of wind
dragging across the states between us.

As hard as the diamonds in your smile,
　　the wind carries its hammers with no hands
and sustains a moan with no mouth,

seems to cradle solitude in its rough arms like firewood
　　to be burned in my house as it passes through
and asks, "Where does she sparkle from?"

and tows behind it tumbleweeds and whirlwinds
　　spinning with possibilities—"Perhaps there is a sea
inside her, perhaps untouched waters—

a pool that no one has swum.
　　Maybe her shimmering eyes are evidence
of holiness in a godless world—

who else could have shellacked so perfectly?"
　　This curious wind goes on,
"Or perhaps there is a darkness inside her

that is being shined into every time you talk.
　　Have you ever been lost so deeply
in yourself

that no one could reach in to pull you out?
    You all have spaces, spaces
that you border with secret shores,

surround with motes of dark and cavernous oceans.
    You could distance yourselves with such darkness,
seclude the tender, sacred and vulnerable landscapes

within you from the harsh alarms and pollution
    of a world that has lost its compassion—
make parts of yourselves dead like flowerwreaths

tossed off a ship that was too weighed down, lost
    until someone shines a wrist of light
across large plains and deep waters

onto what has been cast aside too long."
    And so I tell you, across this great land that is full
of empty spaces, I've been watching things spin,

listening to a sort of fury, losing myself
    and finding half of us. I've been travelling
to prepare for this journey toward you—

let me ride a jagged moon across your sky.
    Let me be a surfer of your dark currents.
Let all that darkness soak me,

and let the light, the condensed light,
    guide me to a greater place. And get me there.
And then let me in.

Wonder Twin Powers Activate

The heroics I would pull if you were my partner—

You are form of a clear lake
            and I am form of a diving duck,
      diving into you, carrying some of you
      on my back, onto solid land.

You are form of an ice palace
            and I am form of blackbirds,
      flying through your closets,
      roosting in your crevices.

You are streams of the sky dripping through the rainforest
            and I am a baboon
      who can't get you out of my bristles.

You are a canal that knows a moon's pull
            and I am an escaped gator
      finding my way through your tunnels,
      arriving at a larger paradise that feels like a tide.

I want to be your wonder twin.
Whatever water you are, I am your animal.

Instructions for Using the Tongue

Don't be too careful—
better to be overflowing
with what the tongue can offer.
Sweet generosity returns to your soft mouth.

Be generous but don't be selfless.
We love the selfish tongue—the tongue
that believes itself to be important
moves easily over us.

When speaking, bang the tongue
off ceilings and into ears.
When licking,
                    do the same.

You can build intricate traps
or whittle through walls,
turn a sucker to juice
and name a constellation.
Your tongue holds secrets on its surface, performs
spell-binding dances in the hall of your mouth.
Always pace. Never vent.
Your tongue is a precise instrument.

"Making Love"

As if we could forge it,
    as if we had ovens
that could bake open
        whatever seeds
        are in us.

But could we sweat
    so wonder-
        fully profusely

without the notion
      of "making" something?

If we were to make something
    out of our bodies,
      why not love?
What a great end product
    to sneak up in sweat!

So let's make love with nothing—
      assemble it under bridges and on airplanes—
Let us create a masterpiece
    out of each other's skin—
It will be great art
    and how others would like to frame it!
Let us hang this art
    in the long-halled museums of our memories—
we'll be benefactors of fleshy moments
    that could be admired during our many visits
      in remembrance—

"the subtle craftsmanship!" "the mastery!"
    "entirely breathtaking!"

Even under the keenest criticism,
you will be able to hear that naysayer in you say,
    "each stroke—pure genius."

Coffee

Honey, I hate mornings
    like a dead leg hates a polka.
I need a morning that brings back the word
       glorious,
reinvents it
    so that I can love breaking light again.

    I need you to wake me up—
    be the energy that fills my cup—
    Shake me awake with your wild inside
    till you see my day pop open wide—

    Let the sun shine over our backs
as we roll each other awake.
Let the skies change over us
and the sheets soil underneath—
    and there, my love,
    between the clouds and the dirt,
       let us find that morning,
    that elusive morning,
       where everything is glorious
       and the birds are references to the music
       coming from our bed.

    I want you to be my coffee,
to pour down my throat,
    make a Lazarus out of me.
         Only you can take all darkness
         right the hell out of me.

A Poem for Men to Steal
& Read to their Girlfriends

Whatever words are in me
aren't equal to the great granite walls
that house this bank inside me,
this great cache of feelings
that shine like laser eyes in a sensitive
security system. Here, my feelings for you
are a palm full of jewels and chokers,
garish and delicate. My other hand
a fistful of bank notes, pulled together as tight
as the tissue around my heart.

If only I could tell you—
if only I could steal some
out of this vault—a deposit box
so difficult to make a withdrawal from—
if only I could smuggle some of the gems
you have created in me,
carry them through the tunnel of my throat
into the sunlight between us
where they would glisten, I'm sure,
where we could examine them,
where you could see their worth
does not merely garner interest in me
but is rather what I have based all my checks
and balances on, what I look at in me
when I want to see what heroics, what savings

I should pull off with you. I appraise it everyday—
it is what I value. See, I offer it here,
all my digits open to you, all the security guards watching
to see if your hand withdraws.

For One Who Almost Couldn't Admit It

Now that you've said you love me
have the willows outside your house
tossed themselves into a new frenzy?
For that little bit of opening,
have the ants crawled out of your walls
and piled their crumbs back into any holes
they came across, shutting you & your dwelling
up for good? Will there be no more irises
in your garden tomorrow morning,
or perhaps any rainbows that covet
your roof will melt into Rorschach pastels
in your gutters and birdsongs in your windows
turn into shrill shriekings as you recall
how, for one moment, you were as brave
and equal to beauty as that which you feel?

Can't a world end gloriously?

Poem for My Friends

Tonight the old girlfriends are lingering
in the air, on the undersides of our eyelids, lining
up outside the doors we've closed
on the delicate toes of their needs.
All of us, each of us,
has found a love that's shut them out
for good. My friends, we've been drunk,
broke, beaten together. We've loved
each other as only men can.
So tell me, how did we ever get like this?

I saw it in your eyes, heard in your voices—the movement
of an ancient wind coursing across your smooth bones—
one by one you approached me—
"I'm in love," you each invariably said,
each unsure of what it meant.
I thought you were falling
from me, but now I understand.
I, too, hear those rainsticks,
those windchimes swaying with this strange weather,
that old rattlesnake with a slick flicker
wrapping up my jointed spine
and still rattling.

So let us toast each other and our old lovers—
the girls who let us undress them,
the girls who were patient with our fumbling,
the girls we no longer need
but refer to each time we learn.
May the roads that stretch before them

bend as easily as their curves
folded into our arms—the creases in us
still containing the lamp oil
we were lit beautifully by for a while.

The Apple Orchard in October

Trees discover in their bodies
   a new brightness
their slow, dark wood
held like a secret.
The mountains bumper
this valley and contain
winks of wilderness that are purple
for today.
               Tomorrow,
rainbows will float
from trees and turn
black, become soil,
and these hawks will die,
and we will die,
and everything will become soil,
and there is this moment
singing with color:

  Hurry! Hurry!

and with these mountains nudging
us, you fly
into my widely opened arms.

Dating a Masseuse

Your hands are full of snap-
    dragons and wrap my bones in these soft bells.
From shoulders to butt to calves,

I lay myself out as you swaddle
    all my pain with evidence of softness,
with the fossils of ancient flowers in your fingerprints—

I feel a wind blows in you—you are full
    of wind and bend my stiff wood
towards a lake—

You are the moon pulling my tide
    into your forearms—
You are the warm shadow inside a fist—

If I were bread
    and if you ever kneaded me,
into your palms I would rise.

Under the Elm

We left the party, walked
beneath a moon that seemed
more a spotlight that night,
until we found a tree.
We pressed against it
and the grass rose around us,
the sky continued to darken,
and soon days, weeks, migrations,
and metamorphoses passed
as we kissed ourselves out
of our bored lives.

      Us—two thousand miles away now,
the grass still growing wild
around our feet.

XV

Suzuki Dance

It starts in her body—
    a flame that makes her skin glow
like a lampshade around a belly full of lightning,
        spreads her light
    that is her
        into the world around her—

    yesterday she danced on a stage,
        today a creek,
            tomorrow—
        who knows tomorrow—
    but know she will dance.
There is no stopping this wild and precise woman
    who is moved only by instinct,
        unpolluted by thoughts
      of if and when and how and just
        is,
    with my eyes on her
        like oxygen to her flame—
    she loves a poet's energy around her dance,
      a net to capture the moment
        but release the energy—
she moves quicker now,
          her feet thrust into the creek bed stones—
      a sundance in water,
    movements of a dragon
        picking flowers—

the world, the sky, thoughts of love
                              swinging around her,
          the great conductor's baton
                              keeping her time.

Enchanted, I'm Sure

You're no Cinderella and this is no glass slipper
I offer you—it is a book of poems
which you could probably see through
in severe sunlight like that prince's lucky shoe
(and this might even sparkle in places too)
but still, I remind myself, this is no fairy tale—
our love is not rose petals or pixie dust—
it is dirt and wind-swept boulders and the faded clapboards
of the shabby green house you grew up in,
too small for your sisters and mother and you, and your father
long gone to Vegas and you hoping for some action
from that missing man in the purple snakeskin suit.
I have been to your old house and seen in closets
the lines of sequin dresses your sisters and you
used once or twice, a row of single shiny memories
full of dance and moons and bare shoulders. Tonight,
for the sake of romance, I'd like to swing
into your senior prom where you were stranded by your date
for some Wild Turkey in the parking lot, pick you
out of the crowd of hairdos, Soft Musk and corsages, and spin magic
with you until midnight. No Prince Charming here, you know that—
I'd be your dirty little Elvis and you'd be my Priscilla,
Jailhouse Rocking out of the prisons of childhood pain
and abandonment—transforming that dark cavern of a gym
into a kind of Graceland—you'd dance close with the King
and all subjects we ever knew would bow down to this moment.
Our love, we'd know, is older than stars,
older than fibs and royalty could allow for,
and even the mice beneath the tight floorboards

would be happy that night. And when midnight calls, as it must,
and you and I recede back into rags and sorrow,
I would start my search for you, carrying into the world
what you've left in me—these poems, the thought of this book—
bringing it into villages and mountains and overgrown forests,
shaking up every fuzzy tree and shaking down every barfly
until I came across you, leaning against a screen door somewhere,
shucking pecans and drinking pop—I'd love every inch
of this path to you, from fading dreams to your feet,
kneel down, and know your real name, no fairy tale,
know we were written by a great hand long ago,
and know how this book fits only you.

Words, Love Poems

Words, love poems, bah!—as if the loose-stitched tapestries
    I weave on these pages
could contain the intense light & honed edges
    found in the way I love you.

Tonight, my singular, I find banging words into this page
    to be too like hammering nickels
        into wooden beams—
too imprecise, not sharp enough
    to slip through the stacked tightness
        of aged grains—

how I've felt my feelings slip
    between this book's words
like warm breath through cold fingers—

Tonight, my soon-to-be-distant one,
    I would give you motions, not words—
the precise motion of, say,

ice melting off a shed's tin roof,
    forming pools of its changed, clear self
    in the midst of this sudden heat—

and if that pool grows to a frozen ocean in the frost of distance,
    then an ice cutter's hull, clipping its way
    through a frozen history,
    shattering the cool surface of your eyes—
    ice that could support the weight of my entire body.
    My boat would float through,
    making a path for whatever will follow in you.

Of pens, Shakespeare's, full of rhythm and effortless diction,
    with a big feather at the end—
Or better yet, Neruda's—
      although I only speak English,
      when talking about love I prefer
      to feel my way through the rhythms
      of a language I cannot comprehend.

Of flames, passion.

Of skies, the sky at any time—
      how it is always full of greased movement
      and glides over this land.
      I would circle around your skin
      and continue indefinitely
      the way weather loves a planet.

Of pottery, a vase in the kiln's desert—
      the movement is in the hardening
      into something beautiful, the evolving
      in this great heat into something that can hold
      whatever will be passed between us—
      my movement would last beyond our lifetimes.

Of storms, a long, soft drizzle,
      knocking over nothing
      but softening everything.

Of animals, the book worm
      boring my way through shelves of love poetry,
      still hungry, until I hit the space for this book
      which is not there
      because it has been given to you.

I know these words are not sustenance enough,
     cannot fill the appetite you create in me
        or I in you,
    but know my body is moving
       behind each word—

the way you move me
as my pen reaches the end of this book
is always toward you.
See?   You are holding the trail I've left.

About the Author

BJ Ward lives in Washington, NJ. His first book, *Landing in New Jersey with Soft Hands*, was published in 1994 by North Atlantic Books. He is the recipient of a poetry fellowship from the New Jersey State Council on the Arts/Department of State. In 1991, he earned an M.A. in Creative Writing from Syracuse University where he served as University Distinguished Fellow and University Summer Fellow. He received a B.A. in Literature From Stockton State College in 1989. He currently teaches at Centenary College in Hackettstown, NJ, works in the Writers-in-the-Schools program for the New Jersey State Council on the Arts, and is the Poetry Instructor at Middlesex County Arts High School in New Jersey.